AN ARCHAIC RECORDING SYSTEM AND THE ORIGIN OF WRITING*

by

Denise Schmandt-Besserat
Center for Middle Eastern Studies
The University of Texas at Austin

A recording system based on tokens, spread throughout the Near East from the early Neolithic on, is proposed as a demonstrable antecedent of the cuneiform writing system. Consisting of a rich and differentiated repertory of shapes and markings, this token system is more complex than a simple system of un-differentiated counters. A first attempt at an inventory of the most representative shapes of tokens from throughout the Near East is provided, including all the documentation presently available to me. On this basis a preliminary comparison is made with signs found on the earliest tablets, and an interpretation is suggested for the identification of some of the existing tokens. Finally, a developmental scheme is proposed to explain the transition from tokens and bullae as prototypes of writing to a full-fledged writing system of impressed and incised signs.

Table of Contents

1. Some Characteristics of the Early Tablets   2
2. A New Hypothesis   3
3. An Inventory of Clay Tokens   3
4. The Function of the Clay Tokens 22
5. The Evolution from Tokens to Tablets 25
6. Conclusions 27
   References 28
   List of Credits 32
   Plates I-VIII (=Figs. 1-9) . . . . after p. 16

---

* This article is the result of a study sponsored by the Radcliffe Institute in 1969-71 and a travel grant to study early clay object collections in the Middle East by the Wenner Gren Foundation (grant no. 2684, 1970). I would like to give special thanks to Giorgio Buccellati whose expertise as an Assyriologist as well as an editor contributed to the overall clarity and organization of the text. I am indebted to Ellen Simmons for the drawing of all the illustrations, maps and charts.

1. Some Characteristics of the Early Tablets

The origins of writing are still surrounded with mystery. All we know is that writing first appears in Mesopotamia but the date remains only approximated to 3500-3000 B.C. ad it is disputed whether the Sumerians or rather the Subarians (their predecessors in upper Mso-potamia) are the inventors. Writing is assumed to have evolved from a first pictograph stage where each word is represented by a small picture or logogram, to the elaborate cuneiform script where the characters, or phonograms, represent sounds. We base our prent knowledge of the beginnings of writing on a body of around 1500 texts recovered in Wark (1000), Jemdet Nasr (200), Kish, Nippur, Godin Tepe, Jebel Aruda, and Habuba Kabira. (The Tartaria tablets are not considered here because of their peculiar typological features and questionable chronological attribution.) The content of the texts is for the greatest part still enigmatic to epigraphists but there is strong indication that they were administrative records of economic activities. The seal impressions they bear confirm their official use.

The early texts have a number of enigmatic features.

1. The signs belong to two types:

    (A) Pictographs which depict in a readily recognizable fashion the objects they stand for. This type is rare and represents a vocabulary of infrequent use such as chariot, variety of birds, wolf, etc..

    (B) Totally abstract signs which cannot be understood by the non-initiated. This second category constitutes the great majority of the signs (which explains why most of the tablets are still undeciphered). It is important to note that while some characters assume totally odd shapes, series consist of multiple variations of basic forms including circles, cones and rods (Fig. 1). Indeed, among 950 signs compiled by Falkenstein from the Warka tablets, 107 (11%) are variations on circles, semi-circles, ovals, etc.; 96 (10%) are variations of cones and diamonds and 42 (4%) are rods of various sizes and bearing different striations and appendices.[1] The abstract signs which have so far been under-stood represent commodities of current usage; for instance the sheep is represented by a circle enclosing a cross, bread by a cone with an incised line parallel to the base, oil by a cone with a convex base, and beer by a cone with a constriction above the base. Numbers are also represented by variations of cones and circles which are differentiated from the remaining vocabulary by the technique of impressing them with the blunt part of the stylus while the other characters are incised with the pointed tip.

2. The repertory of the first signs unexpectedly consists of a sophisticated and impressive vocabulary estimated to consist of around 2000 words.[2]

3. Although the sites where the early texts have been recovered are scattered over a wide area extending from Warka in Mesopotamia to Habuba Kabira in Syria and Godin Tepe in Iran, the signs used are mostly identical and evidence a rapid, if not instant, standard-ization.

4. Except for land sales which are usually written on stone tablets (Figs. 2a,b), the early texts are usually written on tablets made of clay—an impractical material in some respects,

---

[1] A. Falkenstein. *Archaische Texte aus Uruk.* Ausgrabungen der Deutschen Forschungsgemeinschaft in Uruk-Warka, Deutsche Forschungsgemeinschaft, Berlin 1936.

[2] *Ibid.,* p. 29.

since it smears easily, it does not allow for an easy impression of curved lines and it requires an extended drying or firing process before circulation (Fig. 3).

The abstract character of the signs, the extensive repertory of vocabulary, and its immediate standardization seem to indicate that, as we have it, it was already a well developed and sophisticated writing system, not a humble beginning. Some epigraphists have suggested that prior to the tablets an earlier phase of writing may have existed, possibly practiced on a perishable material which has not survived. I am inclined to think that the shape of the abstract signs and the choice of material of the tablets may be leads to an earlier prototype for which I believe I can adduce concrete evidence.

2. A New Hypothesis

In 1966, Pierre Amiet identified in the archives of Susa an archaic system of recording dating from the second half of the Fourth Millennium B.C., and slightly predating the earliest tablets.[3] The system consists of small clay tokens of geometric shapes mostly in the form of spheres, discs, cones, and tetrahedrons, found enclosed in clay envelopes in the shape of hollow clay balls (called "*bullae*") (Fig. 4). The surface of the *bullae* usually bears seal impressions and sometimes marks indicating the number of tokens enclosed. Pierre Amiet interprets each *bulla* as representing a transaction, the tokens inside indicating the kinds of goods exchanged by their shapes and the quantity by their size and number. Amiet suggests a possible relationship between the tokens and the earliest writing, and in particular between the shape of the abstract signs and the shape of the tokens.

In the course of my recent study on the earliest uses of clay in the Middle East, I found that geometric tokens (Fig. 5-6) identical to those identified by Pierre Amiet in the *bullae* are actually found in *most* Middle Eastern sites and over a long span of time, from the ninth to the second Millennium B.C..[4] I was also able to establish the existence of a complex typological inventory of shapes, the internal structure of which is brought to light by the similarity of the shapes of the tokens with some of the early abstract signs, particularly the numerical signs and several representing some of the most usual commodities. In the present paper I will first provide a documentation for the system of tokens and will then describe four stages in the evolution from the early recording system based on tokens to actual writing as known from tablets.

3. An Inventory of Clay Tokens

3.1. Shapes

The tokens come mostly in four broad types of shapes including: I. Spheres, II. Discs, III. Cones and Tetrahedrons, IV. Cylindrical Rods. Each category can be divided into a series of subtypes as illustrated in Chart 1.

---

[3] Pierre Amiet. "Il y a 5000 ans les Elamites inventaient l'écriture," *Archéologia* 12:20-22, 1966.

[4] For earlier reports on my findings see Denise Schmandt-Besserat, "The Use of Clay before Pottery in the Zagros." *Expedition* 16, 2, 1974; "The Earliest Uses of Clay in Syria," *Expedition* 19, 3, 1977; and "The Earliest Uses of Clay in Turkey," *Anatolian Studies* 27, 1977.

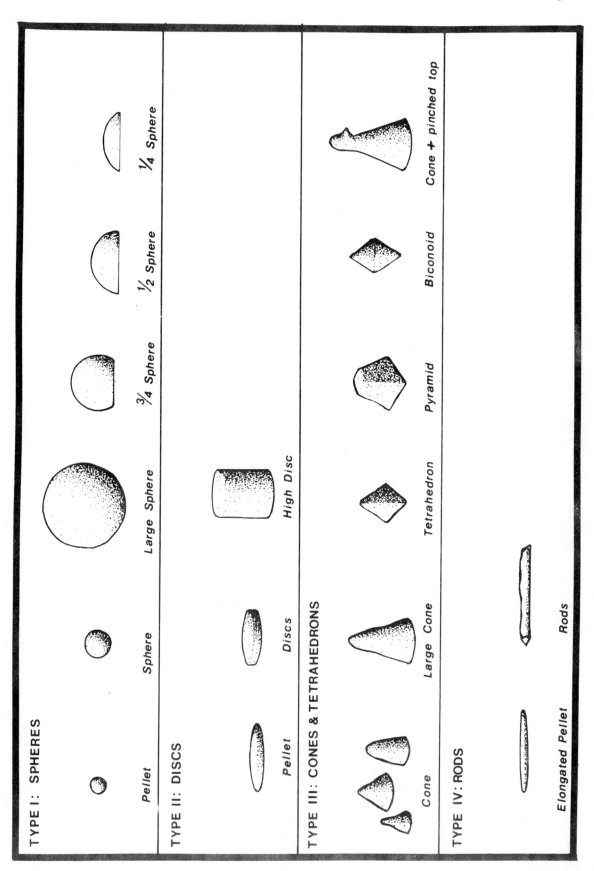

Chart 1
Geometric Objects

Type I: Spheres

The spheres are usually nicely spherical but as they are modelled between the palms of the hands, many examples show a tendency to be somewhat flattish or ovoid and others are faceted. The surface is usually very smooth, suggesting that they were made with wet clay which produced a self slip. There are, however, examples which exhibit a rough, uneven surface, including cracks. On occasion there are traces of the material they were laid upon to dry, such as straw or textile.

The spheres can be divided into 11 different subtypes according to size, fraction and surface markings such as incisions and punches.

1. Pellets

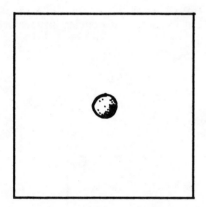

Size: 5 mm. in diameter and less

Distribution: Tepe Asiab, Ganj-Dareh Tepe, Sarab

Number: at least 61 at Asiab

2. Spheres

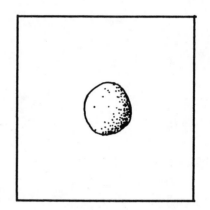

Size: 6 mm. to 2.5 cm. with maximum frequency 1-1.5 cm.

Distribution: most common type of geometric objects found in virtually all early Near Eastern sites; present in Khartoum

Number: 1153 at Jarmo

3. Large Spheres

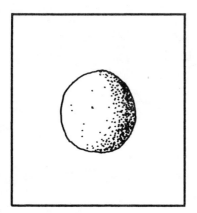

Size: larger than 2.5 cm.

Distribution: Ganj-Dareh Tepe, Tepe Guran, Tell Abu Hureyra

4. Incised Spheres

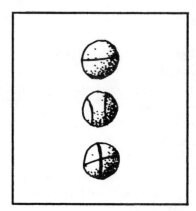

Size: 6 mm. to 2.5 cm.

Distribution: Khartoum, Jarmo, Ur, Susa, Tepe Hissar

Description: bear incisions probably practiced with a pointed stick or bone awl

Patterns: a circle or spiral around the maximum diameter; two circles or spirals on either side of the maximum diameter; two circles intersecting at right angles

5. Punched Spheres

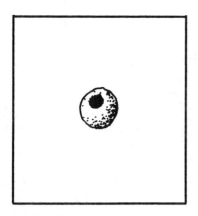

Size: ca. 2 cm.

Distribution: Tepe Asiab, Ganj-Dareh Tepe, Tepe Guran

Description: bear a deep punch probably applied with the blunt end of a stick

6. 3/4 Spheres

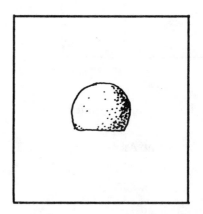

Size: ca. 2 cm. in diameter and 1.5 cm. high

Distribution: Cayönü Tepesi, Ganj-Dareh Tepe, Tepe Sarab, Jarmo, Chaga Sefid, Susa

Description: one flat side achieved by applying pressure on a wet ball against a flat surface

Chart 2. Spheres

Region	Site	I.1	I.2	I.3	I.4	I.5	I.6	I.7	I.8	I.9	I.10	I.11
Iran	SUSA		●		●		●	●				
	TEPE YAHYA		●									
	TAL-I-IBLIS		8									
	ANAU		●									
	TEPE GURAN		●	●		●						
	ALI KOSH		20									
	HAJJI FIRUZ		●									
	SEH GABI		●									
	CHAGA SEFID		19				2	2				13
	TEPE SARAB	●	●	●			●		●		●	
	GANJ DAREH TEPE	●	●			●	●		●		●	
	TEPE ASIAB	●	●			●			●		●	
Mesopotamia	KISH		●				●		●		●	
	TELL ES SAWWAN		●									
	ARPACHIYAH		●									
	GIRD ALI AGHA			1								
	JARMO	←	1153 →		40		20	●	70	16	●	●
Anatolia	BELDIBI		3									
	CAN HASAN		2							1		
	SUBERDE		6									
	CAYÖNÜ TEPESI		●				●					
Syria	TELL ABU HUREYRA			●								
	TELL ASWAD		●									
	TELL RAMAD		2									
Palestine	AIN MALLAHA		●									
	MUNHATTA		●									
	JERICHO											
Egypt	ABYDOS		●									
	KHARTOUM		16		10							

7. Incised 3/4 Spheres

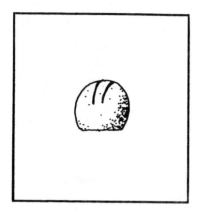

Size: same as above

Distribution: Chaga Sefid, Susa

Description: bear incisions either on the flat or on the convex part

Pattern: two circles on either side of the maximum height

8. Hemispheres

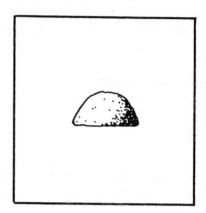

Size: ca. 1.5 cm. in diameter and 7 mm. high

Distribution: Tepe Asiab, Ganj-Dareh Tepe, Tepe Sarab, Jarmo, Kish.

Description: shape achieved by pressing a clay ball against a flat surface; no trace visible of cutting; convex side usually nicely spherical and smooth

9. Incised Hemispheres

Size: same as above

Distribution: Jarmo

Description: bear incisions on the convex side

Pattern: diagonal lines

10. 1/4 Spheres

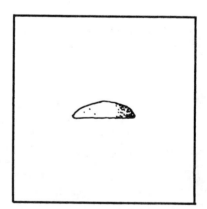

Size: ca. 1.5 cm. in diameter and 3 mm. thick

Distribution: Tepe Asiab, Ganj-Dareh Tepe, Tepe Sarab, Jarmo, Can Hasan, Kish

Description: plano convex disc, very close to type II.1

11. Incised 1/4 Spheres

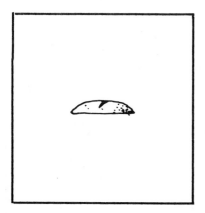

Size: same as above

Distribution: Jarmo, Chaga Sefid, Ur

Description: bear incisions on the convex surface

Pattern: diagonal lines; two lines meeting at
    right angles

Type II: Discs

The discs may be divided into eight different subtypes according to their thickness and the different markings, including incisions and punching.

1. Flattened Pellets

Size: 1-4 cm. in diameter and 5 mm.-1 cm. thick

Distribution: Khartoum, Tepe Asiab, Ganj-Dareh
    Tepe, Çayönü Tepesi, Tepe Guran, Tepe Sarab,
    Tell Ramad, Chaga Sefid, Can Hasan, Seh Gabi,
    Susa

Description: made by squeezing a pellet between
    the fingers; tapering sides, usually with irregular
    contours; uneven thickness and coarse surface

2. Incised Flattened Pellets

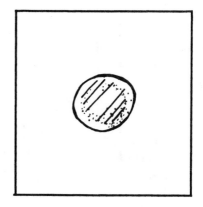

Size: 35 mm. in diameter and 7 mm. high

Distribution: Susa

Description: bear incisions on one side

Pattern: six parallel lines arranged in two rows
    of three lines

	KHARTOUM	ABYDOS	TELL RAMAD	CAYÖNÜ TEPESI	CAN HASAN	BELDIBI	JARMO	JEMDET NASR	KISH	TEPE ASIAB	GANJ DAREH	TEPE GURAN	TEPE SARAB	CHAGA SEFID	TEPE YAHYA	SEH GABI	SUSA	
II.1	7		1	●	1		206			●	●	●	●	2		●	●	
II.2	6																●	
II.3				●	2	7	↓	●	●		●	●	●	3	●		●	
II.4											●						●	
II.5														●			●	
II.6												●						
II.7												●						
II.8											●							
	Egypt		Syria	Anatolia			Mesopotamia			Iran								

Chart 3. Discs

3. Discs

Size: ca. 1.5 cm. in diameter and 1 cm. thick

Distribution: Beldibi, Ganj-Dareh Tepe, Çayönü Tepesi, Tepe Guran, Tepe Sarab, Can Hasan, Chaga Sefid, Tepe Yahya, Susa, Tepe Hissar

Description: straight sides; both circular surfaces slightly concave from pressure between fingers during manufacture; usually very carefully made

4. Incised Discs

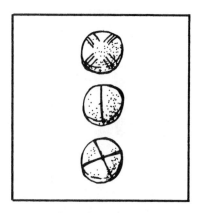

Size: same as type 3

Distribution: Ganj-Dareh Tepe, Susa

Description: bear incisions on one side

Patterns: small strokes around the edge; one line in the center; two lines meeting at right angles in the center; series of parallel lines

5. Punched Discs

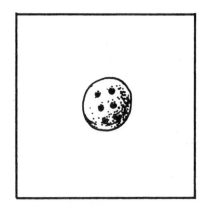

Size: same as type 3

Distribution: Tepe Sarab, Susa

Description: bear punched marks on one side

Patterns: one punch in the center; six punches in two rows

6. Incised and Punched Discs

Size: same as type 3

Distribution: Ganj-Dareh Tepe

Description: bear incisions and punched marks

Patterns: punch marks in the center; incisions at the periphery

7. High Discs

Size: 7 mm.-1.5 cm. in diameter and 1-1.5 cm.
  high

Distribution: Ganj-Dareh Tepe

Description: short cylinder with straight or
  slightly convex sides

8. Incised High Discs

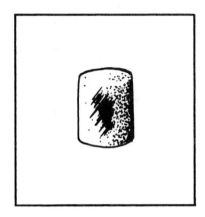

Size: same as above

Distribution: Tepe Asiab

Description: bear deep incision along the side

Type III: **Cones and Tetrahedrons**

This category contains the most popular and numerous shapes after the spheres. The majority
of the examples are carefully made with fine clay. Twelve subtypes have been identified.

1. Cones

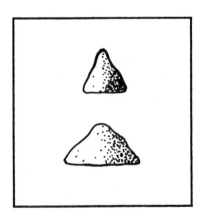

Size: 1-3 cm. high; 1-2.5 cm. base diameter,
  usually 1.5 cm. high and 1 cm. base
  diameter

Distribution: Tepe Asiab, Ganj-Dareh Tepe,
  Cayönü Tepesi, Tepe Sarab, Tepe Guran,
  Jericho, Jarmo, Suberde, Tell Aswad, Tell
  Ramad, Belt Cave, Hajji Firuz, Anau, Seh
  Gabi, Can Hasan, Tell es Sawwan, Tepe
  Gawra, Arpachiyah, Tal-i-Iblis, Susa, Tepe
  Hissar, Tal-i-Bakun, Tepe Yahya, Ur, Kish,
  Megiddo, Abu Hammam

Description: many variations including squat
  or high examples; round or pointed tips;
  usually slightly concave sides; round to oval
  base sometimes slightly concave

2. Large Cones

Size: 3-5 cm. high and ca. 2-2.5 cm. at the base

Distribution: Ganj-Dareh Tepe, Cayönü Tepesi, Chaga Sefid, Tepe Yahya

Description: usually asymmetrical with the top bending in one direction; often carelessly made

3. Cones with a Rounded Base

Size: 1-2 cm. high and 1-1.5 cm. base diameter

Distribution: Tal-i-Bakun, Susa

Description: convex base in the shape of a pear or drop. There is often an incision running around the maximum diameter

4. Cones with a Constriction Above the Base

Size: same as type 1

Distribution: Tepe Sarab, Tepe Guran, Susa

Description: deep groove or circular incision above the base often performed with fingernail

5. Incised Cones

Size: 2.5 cm. high and 2-2.5 cm. base diameter

Distribution: Ganj-Dareh Tepe, Cayönü Tepesi, Tepe Sarab, Suberde, Susa

Description: bear incised marks on the side

Patterns: deep groove in a saw-tooth pattern penetrating 3-5 mm. inside the cone, made by pushing a stick back and forth; rarely, decorative motifs such as herringbone patterns

Region	Site	III.1	III.2	III.3	III.4	III.5	III.6	III.7	III.8	III.9	III.10	III.11	III.12
Iran	SUSA	●		●	●	●	●		●	●		●	●
	TAL-I-BAKUN												
	TAL-I-IBLIS	10											
	TEPE YAHYA	●	●										
	ANAU	●							●				
	TEPE GURAN	●			●								
	HAJJI FIRUZ	●											
	SEH GABI	●	2						●				
	CHAGA SEFID												
	TEPE SARAB	●			●	●			●				
	BELT CAVE	5											
	GANJ DAREH TEPE	●	●			●	●		●		●		●
	TEPE ASIAB	●					●						●
Mesopotamia	KISH	●											
	UR	●											
	TELL ES SAWWAN	●											●
	ARPACHIYAH	●											
	TEPE GAWRA	●											●
	JARMO	106 →							20				
Anatolia	CAN HASAN	3										13	
	SUBERDE	33				2						1	
	ÇAYÖNÜ TEPESI	●	●			●			●				
Syria	TELL ASWAD	●											●
	TELL RAMAD						1	1					21
Palestine	ABU HAMMAM	4											
		●											
	MEGIDDO	●											
	JERICHO	●											

Chart 4. Cones and Tetrahedrons

6. Punched Cones

Size: same as type 1

Distribution: Tepe Asiab, Ganj-Dareh Tepe, Tell Ramad, Susa

Description: bear a punch mark usually at the tip or along the side; on one occasion six punch marks on the sides

7. Cone with a Coil

Size: 2 cm. high and 1.9 cm. at the base

Distribution: Tell Ramad, Chaga Sefid

Description: small clay coil wrapped around the base

8. Tetrahedrons

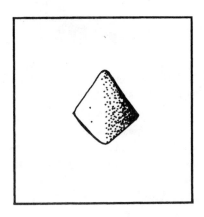

Size: ca. 2.5 cm. at the base and 2 cm. high

Distribution: Ganj-Dareh Tepe, Cayönü Tepesi, Anau, Jarmo, Tepe Sarab, Chaga Sefid, Seh Gabi, Susa

Description: triangular base and three sides defined by more or less sharp edges; tip pointed or round

9. Tetrahedrons with a Constriction Above the Base

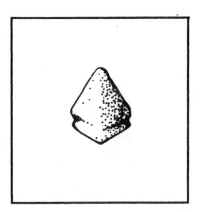

Size: same as type 8

Distribution: Susa

Description: deep groove fashioned with nails above the base

10. Pyramids   **11. Biconoids**

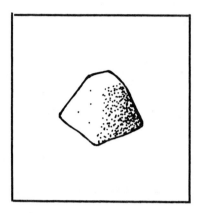

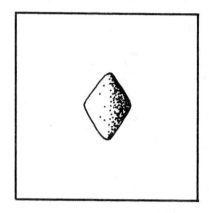

Size: ca. 1.5 cm. high and 2-2.5 cm. at the
   base

Distribution: Ganj-Dareh Tepe, Tal-i-Bakun

Description: square base, four sloping sides
   defined by more or less sharp edges; usually
   flat top

Size: 2.7-2 cm. high and 1.5-1 cm. thick

Distribution: Susa, Ur

Description: two cones joined at the base; usually
   nail incisions emphasize the greatest diameter;
   on one occasion, incised linear pattern on one
   of the two cones

12. Cones with Pinched Tops or Animal Heads (Figure 4)

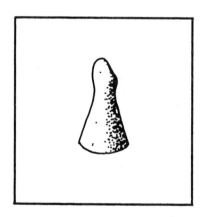

Size: 2-3 cm. high and 2-2.5 cm. at the base

Distribution: Tepe Asiab, Ganj-Dareh Tepe, Tell
   Aswad, Tell Ramad, Suberde, Can Hasan, Tell
   es Sawwan, Tepe Gawra, Susa

Description: tip pinched into a flat squarish end;
   often takes the appearance of a bird's head; in
   other cases looks like an animal or human head;
   details may include pointed muzzle, ears, incised mustache

Type IV: Rods

The shape of these objects makes them particularly fragile and very few have come to us
complete. There are two distinct types, classified according to their manufacture.

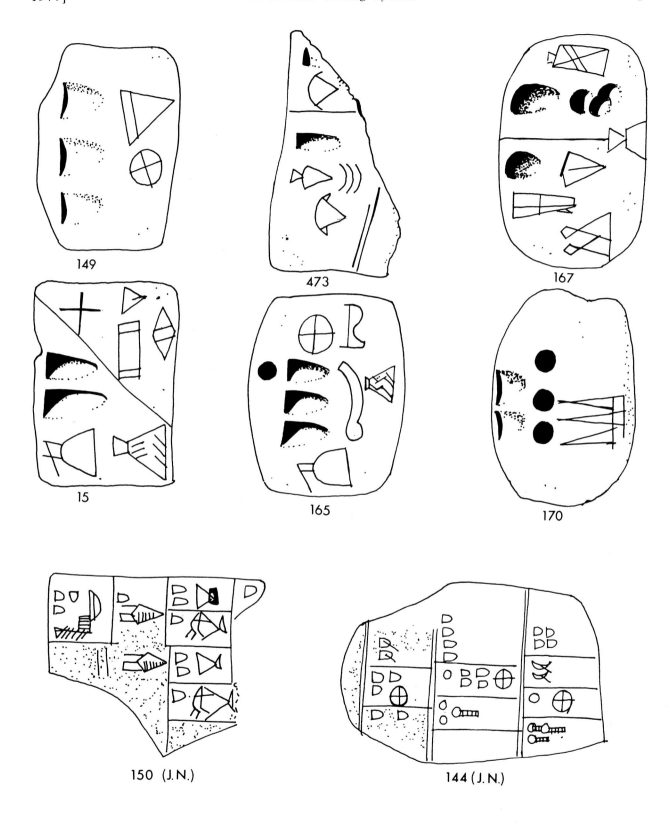

Figure 1. Clay tablets from Warka (149, 15, 167, 170, 473, 165)
and Jemdet Nasr (150, 144)

Figure 2a.
Black stone tablet, obverse, sale of land property.

Figure 2b.
Black stone tablet, reverse.

SMS 1, 49

Figure 3. Clay numerical tablet.
Each conical punch mark stands for 1 unit, the circular one for 10 units.

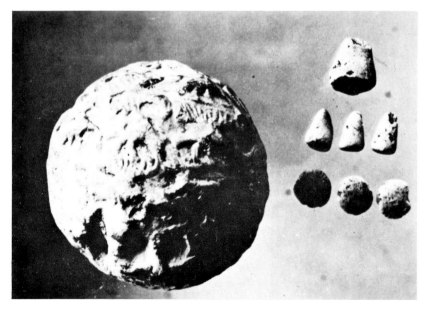

Figure 4. Susa, Iran. Bulla with its contents:
1 large cone, 3 cones, 3 discs. Note corresponding circular
and conical marks on the outside of the bulla.

Figure 5.
Jarmo, Iraq. Spheres, discs, cones and tetrahedrons.

Figure 6.
Tepe Yahya, Iran. Spheres, discs and cones.

Figure 7. Tepe Yahya, Iran.
Bulla with its contents:
1 cone and 2 spheres.
Note the three undifferentiated
marks on the surface of the bulla.

Figure 8. Susa, Iran. Bulla with its contents:
3 discs and 3 elongated pellets.
Note the corresponding marks on the outside of the bulla.

Figure 9.
Discs with an incised cross from Ur.

1. Elongated Pellets

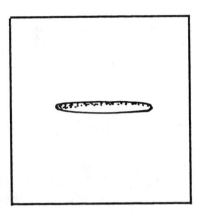

Size: 1.5-5 cm. long and 3 mm.-1 cm. thick

Distribution: Tepe Asiab, Ganj-Dareh Tepe, Tepe Sarab, Chaga Sefid

Description: small coil with tapering ends rolled between the palms of the hands; usually straight, but sometimes curved in a crescent shape

2. Rods

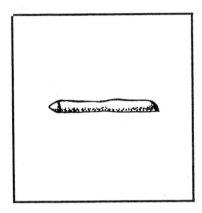

Size: 5 cm. long and 1-1.5 cm. thick

Distribution: Ganj-Dareh Tepe, Tell Abu Hureyra

Description: rods with sharp ends manufactured by cutting a long clay coil to desired length; on occasion coils were achieved by pinching clay on a flat surface giving a triangular section to the rods

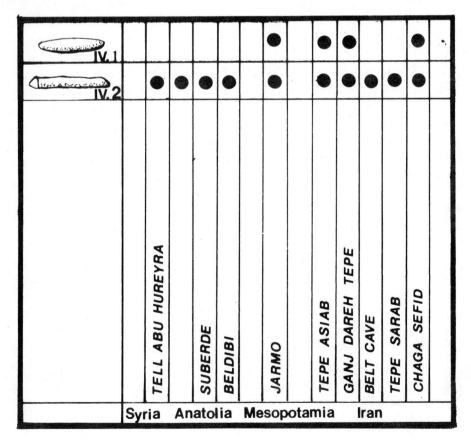

Chart 5. Rods

3.2. Materials

It is noteworthy that the general shape of the tokens is globular. There are no angular shapes represented such as squares, cubes and triangles. This may indicate that the prototypes originated in a soft pliable material such as clay and that tradition perpetuated the habit of modelling them in this material. Indeed almost all the tokens recovered are made of clay. It seems that a very fine clay with rare sand or organic inclusions was generally selected for their manufacture. The clay was usually left untempered.

Rarely are other materials selected for the manufacture of the geometric objects. There is one sphere made of white plaster, recorded at Suberde; five bone discs bearing incisions at Ur; and a unique series of three spheres, seven discs and one cylinder made of red ochre (hematite), at Beldibi. In the IX-VIth millennia, there are few specimens made of stone. Fine colorful stones such as white, pink and black marble and grey slate become popular in later times, for instance at Jemdet Nasr, Kish and Tepe Gawra. The royal cemetery of Ur produced a series of tetrahedrons and cones made of lapis lazuli.

3.3. Manufacturing

The manufacture of the tokens did not involve any mold or particular technique other than hand modelling. No example shows any trace of cutting or abrasion. The spheres, elongated pellets, and cylinders were rolled between the palms of the hands. The 3/4, 1/2 and 1/4 spheres appear to be spheres flattened by applying pressure against a flat surface. The cones, tetrahedrons and discs were shaped between the finger tips. The tetrahedrons involved a slight pressure between three fingers to create the edges. All these shapes are extremely easy to achieve; they are in fact the shapes which spontaneously emerge when doodling with a small lump of clay between the fingers. The tokens usually exhibit regular features and smooth surfaces, which would suggest that the clay used for the manufacture was very soft. The incisions described in the various subtypes and which may confer a special meaning to some cones, spheres and discs, were performed either with the finger nail or with a pointed stick or bone awl. Otherwise there is generally no surface treatment, though occasional burnished specimens occur, and at Susa, two cones appear to have been covered with a red slip.

The general color of the objects is buff, reddish, or red but there are a great number of gray, blackish and black examples. This is the typical range of colors achieved by fired clay. Broken specimens often exhibit a black core, which would suggest that the tokens were fired at low temperatures unable to achieve complete oxidation through the thickness of the objects. This hypothesis was confirmed by a series of tests including DTA (Differential Thermal Analysis) and examination through the scanning microscope performed at MIT under the supervision of W. D. Kingery, on a series of tokens from Tepe Asiab and Tepe Sarab. The tests concluded that a partial fusion of the crystals had occurred, a process which begins at a temperature between 500-700° for Montmorillonite—the type of clay involved.[5]   This

---

[5]Denise Schmandt-Besserat. "The Use of Clay before Pottery in the Zagros." *Expedition* 16, 2:13, 1974.

temperature range is typical of an open hearth and indeed in some instances tokens were found mixed within the ashes of hearths as, for instance, at Tell Ramad. The differences in color would correspond to their location in the hearth during the firing process. The buff and red ones were probably fired on the border where there is much oxygen exchange and the atmosphere oxidizes. The gray and black specimens were at the center where oxygen is rare and the atmosphere reducing. When the geometric objects are executed in stone, they exhibit a superior craftsmanship—the spheres are perfectly round, the cones and tetrahedrons perfectly symmetrical.

3.4. Distribution in Space and Time

The tokens appear in the IXth millennium B.C. (see Chart 6) together with small human and animal figurines and beads, representing the earliest evidence of the use of clay by man in the Middle East. Except for the minute conical flint cores found in quantity for instance at Ganj-Dareh Tepe, there are no objects of similar shape which seem to precede them in the Mesolithic or Paleolithic periods. As was already mentioned above, the globular outline of the general shapes does seem to point to clay for the prototypes.

Tepe Asiab and Ganj-Dareh Tepe are the earliest sites where the tokens occur, and both may be dated to the middle of the IXth millennium B.C. (Ganj-Dareh Tepe, level E 8450± GAK 807). They are present in virtually all Neolithic sites—for instance at Jarmo, Suberde, Anau, Tell es Sawwan and Tal-i-Iblis. They continue in the Bronze Age at Warka, Jemdet Nasr, Tepe Gawra, Kish, the Diyala, Ur, Susa and Tepe Hissar. They are still present in the IInd millennium at Tepe Hissar and Megiddo. There is no evolution to be noticed in the shapes, sizes or types. Vivian Broman notes that at Jarmo tetrahedrons occur when cones become less frequent.[6] This remark does not seem to be true in other sites. There seems to be a greater concentration of tokens in the Zagros and Mesopotamia than in the remaining parts of the Middle East. At Suberde, in Anatolia for instance, the total amount of tokens is 36 cones, 6 spheres and 13 cylinders. This is small compared to the 1153 spheres, 206 discs and 106 cones of Jarmo.[7] Tepe Sarab also has a great number of tokens which are in the process of being inventoried by Vivian Broman. Syria seems to have the fewest, and sites such as Bouqras, Mureybat and Koum have conspicuously yielded none. This may mean either that the tokens were more in demand in Mesopotamia and Iran or that the compact clay archaeological layers of Syria make them especially difficult to find while they are very visible in the sandy fill of the Zagros.

The tokens cover a great spatial extension (see Map 1): they reach Anau and Hissar to the northeast, Bampur and Tepe Yahya to the southeast, Beldibi to the northwest, and Khartoum to the southwest. I also know of their presence in the Francthi cave on mainland Greece.

3.5. Intra-site Clustering

The find spots of the tokens have been carefully plotted in the excavations of Hajji Firuz by Mary Voigt. The publication of the site report is therefore expected to throw light on

---

[6]V. L. Broman. *Jarmo Figurines,* unpublished Master Thesis, Cambridge, p. 58.

[7]*Ibid.,* pp. 62, 63, 58.

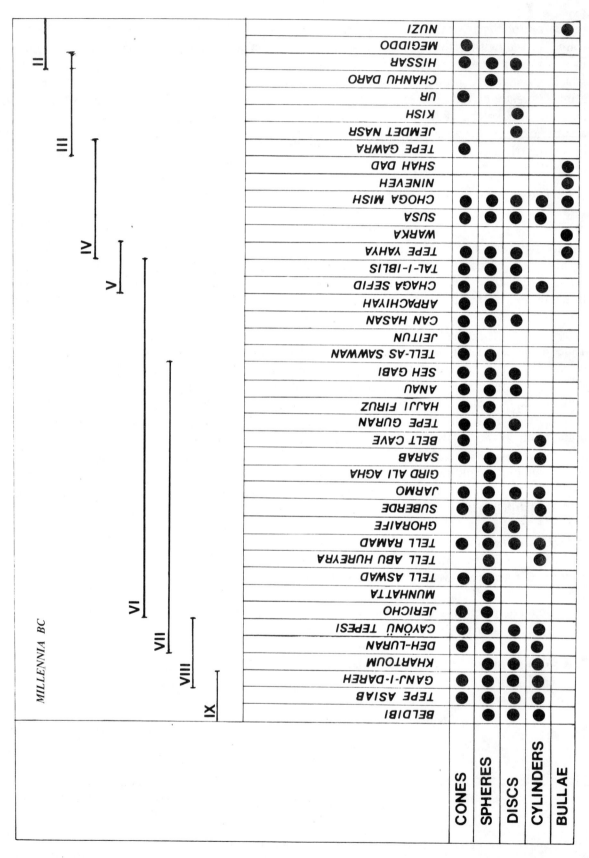

Site	CONES	SPHERES	DISCS	CYLINDERS	BULLAE
NUZI					●
MEGIDDO	●				
HISSAR	●	●	●		
CHANHU DARO		●			
UR	●				
KISH			●		
JEMDET NASR			●		
TEPE GAWRA	●				
SHAH DAD					●
NINEVEH					●
CHOGA MISH	●	●	●	●	●
SUSA	●	●	●	●	
WARKA					●
TEPE YAHYA	●	●			●
TAL-I-IBLIS	●	●	●		
CHAGA SEFID	●	●	●	●	
ARPACHIYAH	●	●			
CAN HASAN	●	●	●		
JEITUN	●				
TELL-AS SAWWAN	●	●			
SEH GABI	●	●	●		
ANAU	●	●	●		
HAJJI FIRUZ	●	●			
TEPE GURAN	●	●	●		
BELT CAVE	●			●	
SARAB	●	●	●	●	
GIRD ALI AGHA		●			
JARMO	●	●	●	●	
SUBERDE	●	●		●	
GHORAIFE		●	●		
TELL RAMAD	●	●	●	●	
TELL ABU HUREYRA		●		●	
TELL ASWAD	●	●			
MUNHATTA		●			
JERICHO	●	●			
CAYÖNÜ TEPESI	●	●	●	●	
DEH-LURAN	●	●	●	●	
KHARTOUM		●	●	●	
GANJ-I-DAREH	●	●	●	●	
TEPE ASIAB	●	●	●	●	
BELDIBI		●	●	●	

MILLENNIA BC — II, III, IV, V, VI, VII, VIII, IX

Chart 6. Time Distribution

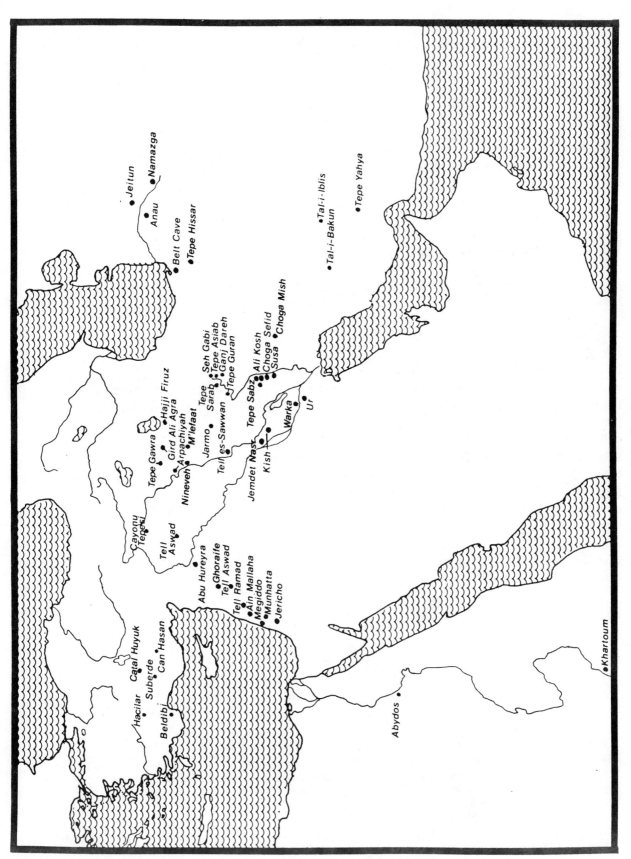

Map 1. Space Distribution

the location of the geometric objects in the houses. In other sites the objects are usually found laying on the floors of houses. They may have a tendency, such as at Tepe Gawra, to concentrate in storage areas. They are found either isolated or in groups of two to five specimens, or, rarely, 15 to 40 at a time. At Tepe Gawra 460 were clustered together.

The tokens may be found in great numbers at certain sites. For instance the inventory made by Vivian Broman for Jarmo lists as stated above 1153 spheres, 206 discs and 106 cones. Unfortunately many sites do not give an accurate count and we are left with vague statements such as in the Tepe Gawra report: "the pieces are virtually ubiquitous."

There is an overwhelming majority of spheres at Jarmo as compared to cones. There also seem to be more spheres at Tepe Asiab, Cayönü Tepesi, Chaga Sefid and Ali Kosh. In contrast, cones are in the majority at Tell Ramad, Suberde, Can Hasan, Ganj-Dareh Tepe and Belt Cave. Discs are predominant at Tepe Guran and Beldibi.

The tokens are usually found loose; if they were kept in containers they must have been baskets or bags made of skin or textile which did not leave any trace.

At a number of sites, including Susa, Tepe Yahya, Shah Dad, Habuba Kabira and Warka, tokens have been found enclosed in hollow clay balls serving as envelopes. These clay balls, called *"bullae,"* are dated to about the first half of the IVth millennium. They are the size of a tennis ball or smaller. They were found totally sealed and had to be broken to identify their contents. The number and type of tokens enclosed has always been variable. For instance, in one case were found one large cone, three small cones and three discs (flattened pellets); in a second, three cylinders (elongated pellets), and three discs; in a third, two spheres and one cone. Some bullae bear the imprint of cylinder or stamp seals impressed upon the entire surface. Some also have a number of punched marks on the outside which repeats the number of items enclosed. At Tepe Yahya, a bulla containing two spheres and one small cone shows three marks (Fig. 7). At Susa, the shape of the punched marks obviously reproduce the form as well as the number of the objects inside (Figs. 4 and 8).[8] A large or small cone is rendered by a conical mark of appropriate size made with the pointed end of a stick or stylus. Discs and spheres are reproduced as a circular mark with the round end of the stylus.[9]

4. The Function of the Clay Tokens

4.1. Epigraphic Evidence from Historical Periods

A *bulla* found at Nuzi may shed some light on the function of the geometric objects.[10] The Nuzi bulla, dated ca. 1500 B.C., was found containing 48 small objects described as

---

[8]Pierre Amiet. "Glyptique Susienne." *Mémoires de la Délégation archéologique en Iran*, Vol. XLIII. Paris 1972. Vol. II, Pl. 61ff.

[9]*Bullae* of the same appearance and covered with undeciphered signs have also been found at Abydos in Egypt. However, they seem to be part of a funerary rite and their content and purpose seem totally different. One series of bullae found in a tomb contained small textile pellets. In another case the content was a tuft of child's hair. T. Eric Peet, "A Remarkable Burial Custom of the Old Kingdom." *The Journal of Egyptian Archaeology* 2:8-9, 1915. Winifred M. Crompton, "Two Clay Balls in the Manchester Museum." *The Journal of Egyptian Archaeology* 3:128, 1916.

[10]The *bulla* is referred to by A. Leo Oppenheim as an "egg-shaped tablet." A. Leo Oppenheim, "An Operational Device in Mesopotamian Bureaucracy." *Journal of Near Eastern Studies* 17:121-28, 1958.

"pebbles" in the report. The *bulla* had the unique feature of bearing on its surface a lengthy cuneiform inscription which referred to the "pebbles" as *abnū* (Akkadian: *abnu*, pl. *abnū*, *abnāti*, counter). The translation of the inscription is the following:

> "*Abnū* (referring to sheep and goats):
> 21 ewes that have given birth
> 6 female lambs
> 8 full grown rams
> 4 male lambs
> 6 she-goats that have given birth
> 1 he-goat
> 2 female kids
> seal of Ziqarru (the shepherd)."

The sum of all the animals mentioned adds up to 48, and there is no doubt that the *abnū* were counters representing animals of a herd. According to A. Leo Oppenheim, there are many instances in which the word *abnū* occurs in short administrative notes and usually it occurs in conjunction with three verbs: "deposit," "transfer" and "remove." Such notes may read "these sheep are with PN; the (pertinent) *abnū* have not been yet deposited;" "three lambs, two young he-goats, the share of PN, they are charged to his account (but) not deposited among the *abnū*;" "one ewe belonging to PN, its *abnū* has not been removed;" "all together 23 sheep of Silwatešup, PN brought . . . their *abnū* have not been transferred;" "x ewes that have lambed, without (pertaining) *abnū*, belonging to PN." These texts suggested to Oppenheim the existence of a system in the Palace of Nuzi of keeping records of the herds by means of small counters. Each animal of the herd was represented by a small object or *abnū* and deposited in a receptacle such as a basket or a pot bearing a mention such as kids, lambs, ewes, rams, he-goats, she-goats, etc.. New *abnū* would be deposited when new animals were born or passed into a new category; *abnū* could be transferred in various receptacles to keep track of change of shepherds or pasture, when animals were shorn, etc.. They would be removed when an animal was traded, died, or was killed for food or sacrifice. Oppenheim interpreted the bulla as a transfer of *abnū* from one account to another, possibly between two different services of the palace. It is interesting to note that the total number of animals did not figure in the inscription, which emphasizes the fact that each category was to be treated separately and deposited in a separate container. This system of accounting was probably widespread in Western Asia and is similar to many early counting systems, in particular, the use of *calculi* in classical times. In fact, Jacobsen notes that Iraqi shepherds still keep account of the animals in their care by means of pebbles.[11] The system of *abnū* could be, and certainly was, applied to accounting for all possible goods. For instance, the Bible pictures Yahweh keeping account of all humans with the same device: all living individuals are represented by a counter in a receptacle. Death occurs when an angel whirls a counter away with a sling.[12]

It seems plausible that the *bullae* found in Mesopotamia and Iran in the IVth millennium had a similar function and were part of a system of accounting as described above. Another very

---

[11]Thorkild Jacobsen, *Human Origins*, Series II, Second Edition, p. 245. University of Chicago Press, 1946.

[12]Otto Eissfeldt, *Der Beutel der Lebendigen*, Berichte über die Verhandlungen des Sächsischen Akademie der Wissenschaften zu Leipzig, Philologisch-Historische Klasse, Band 105, Heft 6, Akademie Verlag, Berlin 1960.

similar interpretation by Pierre Amiet for the *bullae* of Susa is that they were bills of lading accompanying finished products such as textiles, manufactured in the country and transferred to the administrative center in the city.[13] The producer consigned his goods to the care of a middle man together with a bulla containing a number of tokens corresponding to the load of goods. The *bulla* was duly sealed for authentification. The recipient of the load could, by breaking the *bulla,* check the accuracy of the shipment upon arrival.

Transfer of items from one account to the other, bill of lading, the interpretations are certainly not mutually exclusive. In general terms, we may consider the *bullae* as part of an accounting system based on tokens to keep records of transactions. If this assumption is correct, the tokens are counters. Because their presence is recorded throughout the millennia without any evolution of shapes, it may be assumed that this system of recording had its origin in at least the IXth millennium B.C.

4.2. Internal Evidence Based on Comparison with Early Tablets

One crucial point remains to be elucidated: the meaning of all the different shapes of the geometric objects. When the Nuzi *bulla* was found, it was intact and still contained all 48 *abnū,* which in the meantime have unfortunately been separated from the *bulla* and seem irrecoverable. We, therefore, have no information on their material or shapes. Had they been adequately described we may have had the key to whether goats and sheep, kids and lambs, ewes and rams, he- and she-goats were represented by *abnū* of different shapes.

One fact which may be deduced from the Nuzi counters is that each one had the value of one, so that, for instance, the 21 ewes were represented by 21 *abnū*. However, my own conclusion is that such geometric objects as the cones and the spheres (or discs) may have represented different numerical values. I base this hypothesis on the fact that the conical and spherical marks punched outside the *bullae* and obviously representing the cones and spheres (or discs) inside, are identical to the conical and spherical punched signs expressing one and ten on the first numerical tablets (Fig. 8). This would suggest that a first system of recording by the means of counters where a cone stood for one and a sphere (or disc) stood for ten was then complemented by a system of punched marks on the outside of their envelopes, the clay *bullae.* So from the bidimensional syntactical arrangement of the signs on the tablet we can extrapolate to the tridimensional token arrangement of clusters such as are preserved inside *bullae.* The Sumerian signs for one and ten would, in fact, be the pictographs of former *abnū*, probably types III.1 and I.2. It is also important to note that four further signs were used in the early Sumerian arithmetic based on a sexagesimal system: 60 was a large cone; 600 was a cone with an added circular punch; 3600 was a large circle; and 36,000 was a large circle with an added circular punch. All these variations are represented in three dimensions by the geometric objects of types III.2 (large cones), III.6 (punched cones), I.3 (large spheres), and I.5 (punched spheres).

What could be the meaning of the various other shapes of the tokens? Pierre Amiet suggests that they may represent the kinds of items recorded. Amiet bases his hypothesis on the fact that when the earliest pictographs appear, they are generally no longer a true representation

---

[13]Pierre Amiet, *Elam,* Auvers sur Oise, 1966, pp. 70-71.

of the objects, but are already an abstraction.[14]   This would indicate that a previous system had already elaborated a repertory of simplified forms, either in a yet unknown earlier writing on perishable material, or in a system of objects such as the geometric clay objects.

It is certainly very puzzling that the general shape of the series of pictographs on the early tablets from Uruk and compiled by A. Falkenstein[15] are based on variations of conical and spherical forms strikingly similar to specific types of the geometric objects (Chart 7).   For instance, the cones with a constriction above the base (III.4) are similar to Falkenstein's No. 139 which means pitcher.   The cone with a coil at the base (III.7) is similar to sign 535 meaning bread; the cone with a rounded base (III.3) is similar to sign 733 meaning oil. Several unidentified pictographs such as 182, 434, and 526 are similar to shapes III.11, III.6, and III.1.   Other series such as 753-768 are circles filled with linear patterns reminiscent of either the discs or spheres bearing incisions (II.2, II.4, or I.4).   In particular, 761 with a cross enclosed into the circle which means "sheep," is identical to I.4 or II.4 (Fig. 9). Pictographs such as 528-530 are similar to the 1/2 and 3/4 spheres with incisions (I.7 and I.9).   Of course these represent only a few shapes out of the 940 identified by Falkenstein, but what a wealth of information the tokens could reveal if indeed they represent the goods stored, exchanged, traded, or taxed in the early settlements.

5.   The Evolution from Tokens to Tablets

5.1.   The *"Bullae"*

The *"Bullae"* (described above under 3.5) are of great importance because they represent our only evidence that tokens did in fact cluster together according to a specific syntactic system.   One might say that for this early recording system the individual tokens are to morphology what the *bullae* are to syntax.   We are, in other words, beyond the level of representational (or even symbolic) pictography and are conceptually closer to the intrinsic dynamism of writing as a symbolic linkage of symbols.

The *bullae* fulfilled the same function as the early tablets.   They were administrative records of economic transactions.   The former used a three-dimensional system of tokens in the shape of cones, spheres, etc., enclosed *in* a clay ball; the latter used two-dimensional written characters, some in the shapes of cones, spheres, etc., written *on* a clay ball.   The *bullae* could therefore be viewed as the prototypes of the tablets, thereby explaining also the choice of clay for a writing medium.

In developmental terms we may say that the bidimensional system (of tablets) proved more efficient than the tridimensional system of calculi and superseded it.   One might say that the hollow *bullae*, or *bullae* proper, were soon replaced by "full" *bullae, i.e.* tablets, bearing only the numerical signs on their outside.   It is interesting to note in this connection how materials selected to bear the early pictographs vary in the different parts of the world: clay in the Middle East; bone and shell fragments in China; stone architecture in America;

---

[14]Pierre Amiet, "Il y a 5000 ans les Elamites inventaient l'écriture." *Archéologia* 12:16-23, 1966.

[15]A. Falkenstein. *Archaische Texte aus Uruk.* Ausgrabungen der Deutschen Forschungsgemeinschaft in Uruk-Warka, Deutsche Forschungsgemeinschaft, Berlin 1936.

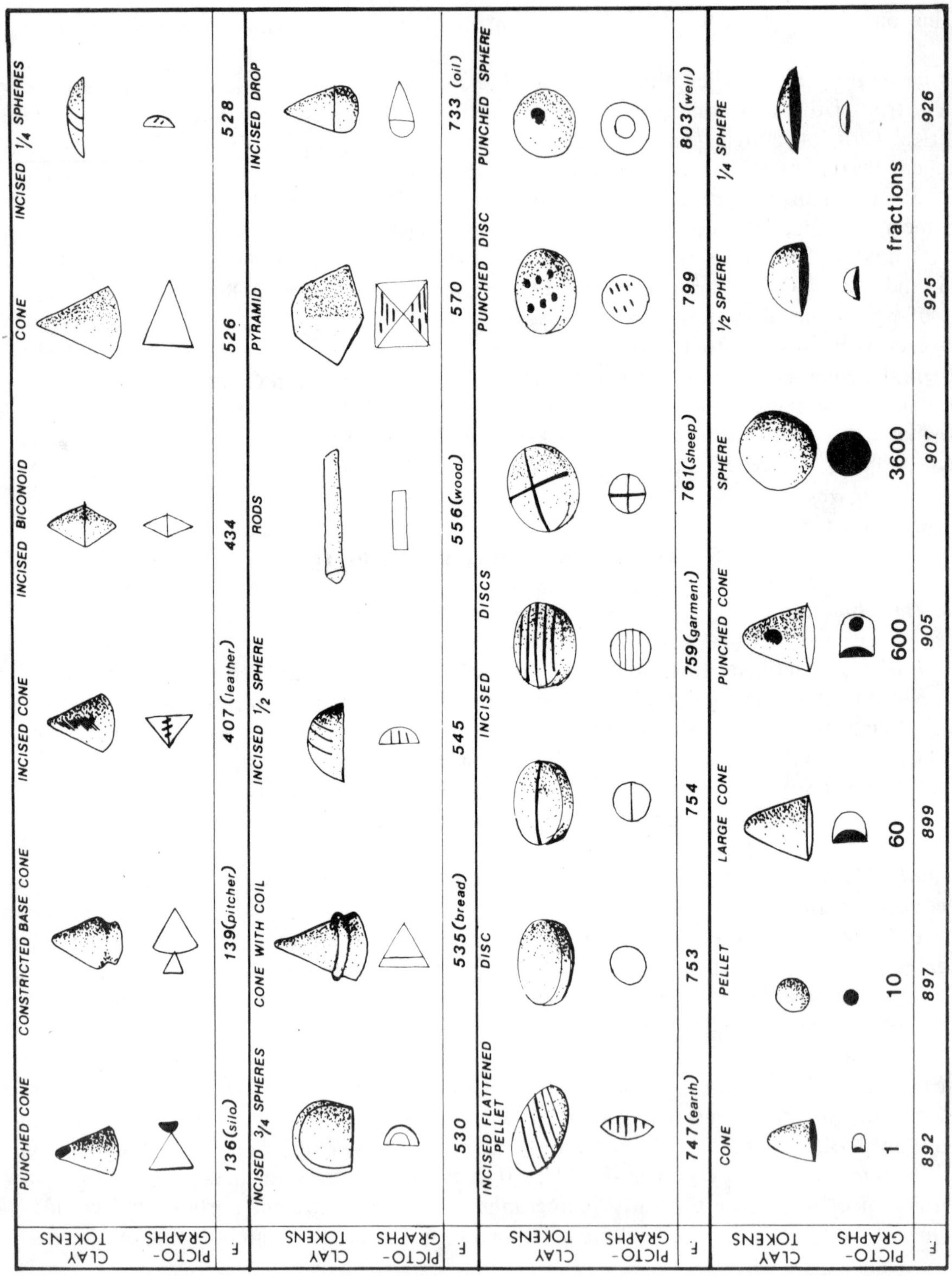

Chart 7

Warka Pictographs and Suggested Corresponding Clay Tokens

*F — See Falkenstein

wooden tablets in the Easter Islands. All are hard material, except for clay. The hard materials required for their preparation the smoothing of a face onto which the signs were incised or carved. The use of clay involved the modelling of a tablet in the shape of a small cushion. The signs were impressed with a stylus, and the documents could not be circulated, certainly presenting some problems in their handling until they had been exposed to the sun or hardened by fire. Why this complicated and time-consuming process? The usual answer is that raw materials such as stone and wood are rare in Mesopotamia. One might also consider that it was perpetuating a tradition beginning with the use of clay *bullae*.

5.2. From Tokens to Signs

The *bullae* provided the great advantage of securing the tokens tightly and presented a surface where seals could be impressed for authentication. Their disadvantage was to totally hide the tokens, thus any verification necessitated the breaking of the *bullae*. To overcome this difficulty some *bullae* bear on their outer surface impressed signs repeating not only the numbers but also the vague shape of the tokens inside: circular impressions for discs and spheres, conical impressions for cones (Fig. 4). The innovation was of course of great convenience as it allowed one to "read" at all times the amount and kind of tokens without breaking the *bulla*. These marks may be viewed as the crucial link between the archaic system of recording in three dimensions and writing. As soon as the system of marks on the exterior of the *bullae* was generally adopted and understood, it obviously made the system of tokens inside the *bulla* superflous and obsolete and tablets with numerical signs made their appearance. At the present stage of my research it appears to me that only a restricted number of token shapes are represented in the *bullae,* in particular those which can be paralleled with numerical signs. If this observation is correct, the *bullae* could have been identical in function to the archaic numerical tablets (Fig. 8), where only numbers were indicated and the goods transferred were evident to the interested parties.

The signs impressed with the blunt tip of a stick did not allow much precision. In particular there was no difference possible between the representation of a sphere or a disc, between a cone and a tetrahedron. Signs incised with a specialized pointed tool or stylus were developed which could render more complicated shapes with accuracy. Though these signs were pictographs, they did not represent the shapes of the items themselves but rather the tokens of the previous recording system. As writing was established, the new vocabulary expressing new inventions such as metal tools, the plough, chariot, etc., consisted of true pictographs, drawn according to the objects themselves.

6. Conclusions

Writing may not have been, as previously assumed, brought by such newcomers to Mesopotamia as the Sumerians, but may represent a new step in the evolution of a sophisticated system of recording which was indigenous to the Middle East since the IXth Millennium B.C.. This accounting system was based on tokens of various geometric and odd shapes. It was used without apparent modifications until the IVth Millennium B.C., when what should have remained a marginal invention, the use of a clay envelope to hold the tokens of a particular transaction and bear the relevant seals, was to thrust the system in a drastically new course.

Check marks noted on the surface of the *bullae* to repeat for convenience the number of tokens inside proved effective and soon supplanted the old system of tokens. If this hypothesis is correct it would shed light on some of the characteristic features of the archaic tablets and in particular their material and often convex forms. It would explain the instant standardization of writing in a widespread area as well as the abstract shapes of all the numerical signs and of a score of commodities of daily use. This theory alters our previous conception of human cultural development. First it pushes back by five millennia the origins of writing. Second it evidences the existence of a sophisticated system of recording prior to writing. Third it suggests the presence of a *lingua franca* in the form of tokens which was shared by a number of prehistoric and early historic cultures of the Middle East and may have extended as far as Nubia and the Indus Valley.

Of course it also raises many more questions, among which some of the more crucial would be what was the prototype of the remaining some 800 signs of the Warka tablets? Which culture of the Middle East from Anatolia to the Zagros invented the token system? How did it become so widespread before any trade is evidenced? Did tokens of identical shapes bear the same meaning in Jarmo and Khartoum? Although they may remain unanswered, these questions are certainly exciting challenges. They will hopefully create a new awareness among excavators and will attract attention to the small, but clearly significant, tokens which up to now have been labeled in site reports as "objects of uncertain purposes."

REFERENCES

Iran

Ali Kosh

HOLE, FRANK *et al.*
   1969   *Prehistory and Human Ecology of the Deh Luran Plain.* Memoirs of the Museum of Anthropology No. 1, p. 226. Ann Arbor: University of Michigan.

Anau

PUMPELLY, RAPHAEL
   1908   *Explorations in Turkestan Expedition in 1904,* I. Washington: Carnegie Institution of Washington.

Tepe Asiab

BRAIDWOOD, R. J., BRUCE HOWE, CHARLES A. REED
   1961   "The Iranian Prehistoric Project." *Science* Vol. 133, No. 3469, pp. 2008-010.

Tall-I-Bakun

LANGSDORF, ALEXANDER and DONALD E. McCOWN
   1942   *Tall-I-Bakun A.* Oriental Institute Publications, No. LIX. Chicago: University of Chicago Press.

Belt Cave

COON, C. S.
   1951   *Cave Exploration in Iran, 1949.* Museum Monographs, p. 75. Philadelphia: The University Museum.

Chaga Sefid

HOLE, FRANK
   n.d.   "Chaga Sefid, Figurines and Objects of Lightly Baked Clay." Unpublished paper, pp. 221-43.

Ganj-Dareh Tepe

SMITH, P. E. I.
    1970   "Survey of Excavations: Ganj-Dareh Tepe." *Iran* 8:174-76.

Tepe Guran

MORTENSON, P.
    1964   "Excavations at Tepe Guran, Luristan II. Early Village-farming Occupation." *Acta Archaeologica* 34:110-21.

Hajji Firuz

YOUNG, T. CUYLER, Jr.
    1962   "Taking the History of the Hasanlu Area Back Another Five Thousand Years: Sixth- and Fifth-Millennium Settlements in Solduz Valley, Persia." *Illustrated London News* Nov. 3:707-19.

Tepe Hissar

SCHMIDT, ERICH F.
    1937   *Excavations at Tepe Hissar, Damghan 1931-33.* Philadelphia: University of Pennsylvania Press.

Tal-i-Iblis

EVETT, D.
    1967   "Artifacts and Architecture of the Iblis I Period: Areas D, F, and G." In *Investigations at Tal-i-Iblis,* ed. J. R. Caldwell. Illinois State Museum Preliminary Reports 9:127.

Tepe Sarab

BRAIDWOOD, R. J., BRUCE HOWE, CHARLES A. REED
    1961   "The Iranian Prehistoric Project." *Science* Vol. 133, No. 3469, pp. 2008-010.

Seh Gabi

YOUNG, T. CUYLER, Jr. and LOUIS D. LEVINE
    1974   *Excavations of the Godin Project: Second Progress Report.* Royal Ontario Museum, Art and Archeology Occasional Paper 26:10.

Susa

DE LA FUYE, ALLOTE, J. T. BELAIEW, R. DE MECQUENEM et J. M. UNVALA
    1934   "Archéologie, Métrologie et Numismatique Susiennes." *Mémoires de la Mission Archéologique Française* 25:193, fig. 28. Paris.

Tepe Yahya

LAMBERG-KARLOVSKY, C. C.
    1970   *Excavations at Tepe Yahya, Iran 1967-69.* Progress Report I, American School of Prehistoric Research, Peabody Museum, Bulletin 27, Harvard University.

Mesopotamia

Tell Arpachiyah

MALLOWAN, M. E. L. and J. C. ROSE
    1935   "Excavations at Tell Arpachiyah, 1933." *Iraq* II:1-178.

Tepe Gawra

SPEISER, E. A.
  1935   *Excavations at Tepe Gawra,* Vol. I. Philadelphia: University of Pennsylvania Press.
TOBLER, A. J.
  1950   *Excavations at Tepe Gawra,* Vol. II. Philadelphia: University of Pennsylvania Press.

Jarmo

BRAIDWOOD, R. J. and BRUCE HOWE
  1960   *Prehistoric Investigations in Iraqi Kurdistan.* Studies in Ancient Oriental Civilizations, No. 3. The University of Chicago Press.
BROMAN, VIVIAN L.
  1958   *Jarmo Figurines.* Unpublished Master's Thesis, Cambridge.

Jemdet Nasr

MACKAY, ERNEST
  1931   *Report on Excavations at Jemdet Nasr, Iraq,* Field Museum of Natural History, Anthropology Memoirs, Vol. 1, No. 3. Chicago.

Karim Shahir

BRAIDWOOD, R. J. and BRUCE HOWE
  1960   *Prehistoric Investigations in Iraqi Kurdistan.* Studies in Ancient Oriental Civilizatons, No. 3. The University of Chicago Press.

Kish

MACKAY, ERNEST
  1925-29   *Report on the Excavation of the "A" Cemetery at Kish, Mesopotamia,* Field Museum of Natural History, Anthropology Memoirs 1:1-2. Chicago.

Nineveh

THOMPSON, R. CAMBELL and M. E. L. MALLOWAN
  1933.   "The British Museum Excavations at Nineveh, 1931-32." *University of Liverpool, Annals of Archaeology and Anthropology* 20:71-186.

Tell es-Sawwan

ABOUL-SOOF, A.
  1968   "Tell es-Sawwan, Excavations at the 4th Season, Spring 1967," *Sumer* 24:3ff.

Shahdad

HAKEMI, ALI
  1972   *Catalogue de l'exposition Lut.* Xabis (Shahdad) Ier Symposium Annual de la recherche Archaeologique en Iran.

Ur

WOOLEY, SIR C. L.
  1934   *Ur Excavations: The Royal Cemetery.* London: Oxford University Press.

Warka

LENZEN, H. J.
  1964   "New Discoveries at Warka in Southern Iraq." *Archaeology* 17, 2:128.

Anatolia

Beldibi

BOSTANCI, E.
    1968   "Beldibi ve Magracikta Yapilam 1967 yaz Mavsimi Kazilari ve Yeni Buluntular." *Turk Arkologi Dergisi* 16, I:58, fig. 3.

Can Hasan

FRENCH, DAVID H.
    1970   "Excavations at Can Hasan: First Preliminary Report." *Anatolian Studies* 20:27.

Cayönü Tepesi

ÇAMBEL, H. and R. J. BRAIDWOOD
    1970   "An Early Framing Village in Turkey." *Scientific American* 3:51-57.

Suberde

BORDAZ, JACQUES
    1969   "The Suberde Excavations in Southwest Turkey, An Interim Report." *Türk Arkeoloji Dergisi,* 17:43-61.

Syria

Tell Abu Hureyra

MOORE, A. M. T.
    1975   "The Excavations of Tell Abu Hureyra in Syria: A Preliminary Report." *Proceedings of the Prehistoric Society* 41:50-77.

Tell Aswad

DE CONTENSON, HENRI
    1972   "Tell Aswad, Fouilles de 1971." *Annales Archéologiques Arabes Syriennes* 22:75-81.

Ghoraifé

DE CONTENSON, HENRI
    1976   "Nouvelles données sur le Néolithique précéramique dans la région de Damas (Syrie) d'après les fouilles à Ghoraifé en 1974." *Bulletin de la Société Préhistorique Française* 73, 3:80-82 C.R.S.M.

Tell Ramad

DE CONTENSON, HENRI
    1971   "Tell Ramad, A Village Site of the VIIth and VIth Millennia B.C.." *Archaeology* 24:278-85.

Ras Shamra

DE CONTENSON, HENRI
    1963   "New Correlations Between Ras Shamra and al-ʿAmuq." *BASOR* 172:35-40.

Palestine

Ain Mallaha

PERROT, JEAN
    1966   "Le Gisement Natoufien de Mallaha (Eynan), Israel." *L'Anthropologie* 70:437-84. Paris.

Jericho

KENYON, KATHLEEN
    1960   *Archaeology in the Holy Land.* London: Ernest Benn.

Munhata

PERROT, JEAN
    1966   "La Troisième Campagne de Fouilles à Munhata." *Syria* 43:46-63.

LIST OF CREDITS

Fig. 2a, b Courtesy of the Yale Babylonian Collection.

Fig. 4   Courtesy of the Musée du Louvre, Paris, France.

Fig. 5   Courtesy of the Peabody Museum, Harvard University.

Fig. 9.   Courtesy of the University Museum, The University of Pennsylvania.

Fig. 10   Courtesy of the Musée du Louvre, Paris, France.

TPR —   N. M. MAGALOUSIS, *et al.*
            "Sourcing Techniques Applied to Soils and Ceramics from Terqa and Dilbat,"
            forthcoming in *SMS*.

TPR —   O. ROUAULT
            "Cuneiform Texts Found at Terqa before the Joint Expedition: A New
            Edition," forthcoming in *SMS*.

TPR —   B. HUFFINE
            "Third Millennium Burials," forthcoming in *SMS*.

TPR —   M. KELLY-BUCCELLATI
            "Seal Impressions from the Third Season," forthcoming in *SMS*.

KPR 1:   O. ROUAULT
            "Soundings at Qraya—The Protoliterate Period," forthcoming in *SMS*.

Ancillary Reports

ARTANES 2:   G. BUCCELLATI and M. KELLY-BUCCELLATI
               IIMAS Field Encoding Manual (Non-Digital). Malibu 1978.

Audio-Visual Modules

DS 1:   G. BUCCELLATI and M. KELLY-BUCCELLATI, Editors
            R. CLAYTON, Systems Director
            General Introduction and the Second Season (Fall 1976). 125 color slides,
            26-minute cassette.

DS 2:   G. BUCCELLATI, M. KELLY-BUCCELLATI and W. R. SHELBY
            Terqa 1977. Malibu 1978.

Documentary Motion Picture

            J. S. MEIGHAN
            By the Meadows of the Euphrates. (21 minutes, color, 16 mm.)

PUBLICATIONS OF THE TERQA ARCHAEOLOGICAL PROJECT

Summary Preliminary Reports

TAP 1:   G. BUCCELLATI and M. KELLY-BUCCELLATI
"The Terqa Archaeological Project: Preliminary Report on the First Two Seasons," forthcoming in *AAS*.

TAP 2:   G. BUCCELLATI and M. KELLY-BUCCELLATI
"The Terqa Archaeological Project: Preliminary Summary Report on the Third Season," forthcoming in *AAS*.

—   G. BUCCELLATI and M. KELLY-BUCCELLATI
New Archaeological Harvests from Syria.   Pasadena 1977.

Modular Preliminary Reports

TPR 1:   G. BUCCELLATI and M. KELLY-BUCCELLATI
"General Introduction and the Stratigraphic Record of the First Two Seasons," *SMS* 1/3 (1977).

TPR 2:   G. BUCCELLATI
"A Cuneiform Tablet from the Second Season," *SMS* 1/4 (1977).

TPR 3:   M. KELLY-BUCCELLATI and L. MOUNT-WILLIAMS
"Object Typology of the Second Season (Excluding Vessels and Lithics)," *SMS* 1/5 (1977).

TPR 4:   M. KELLY-BUCCELLATI and W. R. SHELBY
"Ceramic Vessel Typology of the First and Second Seasons," *SMS* 1/6 (1977).

TPR 5:   A. MAHMOUD
"Die Industrie der islamischen Keramik aus der zweiten Season," *SMS* 2/5 (1978).

TPR 6:   G. BUCCELLATI and M. KELLY-BUCCELLATI
"Chronicle and Stratigraphic Record of the Third Season," *SMS* 2/6 (1978).

TPR —   O. ROUAULT
"Documents épigraphiques de la troisième saison," *SMS* 2/7 (1978).

TPR —   E. GRIFFIN and W. R. SHELBY
"Ceramic Vessel Typology of the Third Season," *SMS* 2/8 (1978).

TPR —   L. MOUNT-WILLIAMS
"Object Typology of the Third Season (Excluding Vessels and Lithics)," *SMS* 3/1 (1978).